I0221549

Leo Michael

She

An Allegory of the Church

Leo Michael

She
An Allegory of the Church

ISBN/EAN: 9783337019853

Printed in Europe, USA, Canada, Australia, Japan

Cover: Foto ©Thomas Meinert / pixelio.de

More available books at **www.hansebooks.com**

SHE

AN ALLEGORY OF THE CHURCH.

NEW YORK:

FRANK F. LOVELL & CO.,

142 AND 144 WORTH STREET,

COPYRIGHT, 1889,
BY JOHN W. LOVELL.

DEDICATION.

TO

THE ONE

WHO TAUGHT ME HOW TO UNVEIL TRUTH

AND MADE ME ACQUAINTED WITH

THE GRAND SECRET OF THE

FIRE OF LIFE,

AND IN WHOSE WORK I BEHOLD THE

PROPHECY OF WHAT "SHE" (THE

CHURCH) IS YET TO BE,

THE AUTHOR GRATEFULLY AND REVERENTLY

DEDICATES

THE FOLLOWING PAGES.

As many as I love, I reprove and chasten : be zealous therefore, and repent.

Behold, I stand at the door, and knock : if any man hear my voice, and open the door, I will come in to him, and will sup with him, and he with me.

He that overcometh, I will give to him to sit down with me in my throne, as I also overcame, and sat down with my Father in his throne.

He that hath an ear, let him hear what the Spirit saith to the churches. Rev. iii. 19–22.

The scholar is unfurnished who has only literary weapons. * * * He will have to answer certain questions, which I must plainly tell you cannot be staved off. For all men, all women, time, your country, your condition, the invisible world, are the interrogators : *Who are you ? What do you ? Can you obtain what you wish ? Is there method in your consciousness ? Can you see tendency in your life ? Can you help any soul ?*

EMERSON.

understand Truth. Amid the ruins of Kor to which Leo penetrated was a beautiful statue carved out of pure white marble, representing the winged figure of a woman of wondrous loveliness. She was bending forward and poising herself upon her half-spread wings as though to preserve her balance as she leaned; her arms outstretched as though about to embrace one she dearly loved, while her whole attitude gave an impression of the tenderest beseeching. Her perfect and most gracious form was naked save the face, which was thinly veiled, so that it was difficult to trace the marking of the features. A gauzy veil was thrown about the head, and, of its two ends, one fell down across her left breast, which was outlined beneath it, while the other streamed away behind her upon the air. The pedestal on which she rested was a huge round ball of stone and the whole was to represent Truth standing on the world,

calling to her children to unveil her face.
At the foot of the statue was the following
inscription :

*Is there no man that will draw my veil
and look upon my face, for it is very fair?
Unto him who draws my veil shall I be, and
peace will I give him, and sweet children of
knowledge and good works.*

*And a voice cried: " Though all those
who seek after thee desire thee, behold ! Vir-
gin art thou, and Virgin shalt thou go till
Time be done. No man is there born of
woman who may draw thy veil and live, nor
shall be. By Death only can thy veil be
drawn, Oh Truth."*

*And Truth stretched out her arms and
wept, because those who sought her might not
find her, nor look upon her face to face.*

Now to the wise these words have other
meaning than that which first presents itself,
and in reading this hidden wisdom lies the
interpretation of " She." To know the per-

fect Truth, to unveil all her divine beauty and have her as thine own bride, you must first die and pass into eternity. But to do this it is by no means necessary to wait for what we have called death. It is possible to be dead to sense even in life, and to find the *eternal now*, in which there are neither to-morrows nor yesterdays, in what men have called time. To acknowledge and live no more after the flesh, but after the Spirit, is to take Truth for your bride.

This is the mystery of Godliness—God-like-ness.

Know yourself as the Christ did—as Spirit. Deny the truth of the false, and the reality of the unreal. Let this outer sense-life be nailed to the Cross until you say " It is finished." This is the simple way of Truth, and yet I cannot say it is easy. No one who is earnest need miss the way, and yet it is true that many are called, but few chosen. There is a way that seemeth right unto man, but the end thereof is death. This is the way of sense. The way of Spirit is the death of sense. This is the one lesson of the Cross of Christ—its Alpha and Omega.

Who of those who call themselves Christians have unveiled this Truth?

As I look out over the earth I see, here and there, one who has read the secret, and, with the light of the eternal morn flashing upon upturned faces, eager hands are about to rend away the last thin veil that obscures to our world the full beauty of Truth. This is the veil that must be rent in twain before any can pass into the Holy of Holies, and stand face to face with Truth.

The ruined City of Kor represents the modern world, and "She" the Church—who has become the sole guardian of Truth without knowing its full meaning, and possessor of the Secret of Eternal Life without dispensing it.

The origin of "She" is shrouded in mystery. How she came to this strange country she tells us not. So also is there a cloud of mystery hanging about the beginning of the Christian Church. Back of Christianity stands Judaism. In conversation with Holly concerning the Jews, "She" said: "They broke my heart, and made me look with evil eyes across the world, and drove me to this wilderness. When I would have taught them wisdom in Jerusalem they stoned me, ay, at the gate of the Temple, those white-bearded hypocrites and rabbis hounded the people on to stone me."

Back of Judaism is Egypt and Moses learned in all its wonderous lore. The Greeks and Egyptians interchanged their knowledge. Pythagoras and Plato both studied in Egypt. From Egypt we are led back across the centuries into a still greater antiquity—to races and civilizations more wonderful than any that exist to-day, and

that have totally disappeared.   Back of the
Christian Church we find also the schools
of the Essenes and earlier Gnostics.   All our
Christian ceremonies are a mingling of
Egyptian, Pagan, and Jewish rites with the
new and truer methods taught by Jesus.

I do not wish to go into historic particu-
lars, for I am in search of the Spirit rather
than of the letter.   When " She " bathed
in the Fire of Life her veins were filled
with jealousy—as she declares, just before
entering the second time.   " When first I
tasted of its virtue, full was my heart of pas-
sion and of hatred of that Egyptian Ame-
nartas, and therefore, despite my strivings
to be rid thereof, have passion and hatred
been stamped upon my soul from that sad
hour to this.   But now is my mood a happy
mood, and filled am I with the purest part
of thought, and so would I ever be."

Passion filled her veins because she was
in love with the outward form of this hand-

some Greek priest of Isis, and for two thousand years she lived in the tombs of Kor, worshipping his dead body. Herein is most wonderfully symbolized the weakness of the Church. It has debased a pure spiritual love with physical passion. It has hovered and gloated over the body, suffering and death of the Jesus rather than lifting up its thought and love to the eternal Christ. Physical passion, physical blood—our theology is incarnadined and saturated with gore. Our Catholic churches and all Christian art repeat over and over every horrible detail of the physical sufferings of Jesus and cloud thereby the spiritual and redeeming power of the Truth he taught. Every Good-Friday we nail his body again to the tree, every Easter we take it out of the tomb, every Christmas we think more of the miracle of his birth than of the Truth he came to make manifest. This error was in the viens of the Church when, as embodied in Juda-

ism, ecclesiastical passion and envy slew
Jesus. They looked for a physical re-
deemer; one who should free them from
the Roman yoke; but his kingdom was
spiritual.

" She " offered Kallikrates the charm of
external beauty made undying. So the
Jews offered Jesus external power and tri-
umph. As Kallikrates turned to the love
of his soul (Amenartas), so did Jesus turn
to his spiritual ideal, saying, " My king-
dom is not of this world. To this end have
I been born, and to this end am I come into
the world, that I should bear witness unto
the Truth." He had rent from Truth the last
veil that obscured her matchless and radiant
face. Living, yet was he dead unto the
flesh. No one could convince him of sin.

Why, then, did he die? Ah, the blind-
ness of our mortality! Following out the
vain imaginings of external intellect, many
occult students have taught that Jesus had

to die because he was capable of anger,
citing the instance of the fig tree—not see-
ing the purely spiritual import of his words
in relation to that incident.

Why did he, over whom death had no
power, die? Because no one would have
believed he had conquered death unless he
had demonstrated it after some such man-
ner as he did, by permitting them to crucify
him and then rising from the tomb. He
taught publicly that there was no need to
die if we would die unto the flesh while yet
living, and live only unto the Spirit. " Who-
soever liveth and believeth in me shall
never die." " If a man keep my saying he
shall never taste of death."

This was too good news to believe, and
to give possibility to faith, he said, " Destroy
this temple (meaning his body), and in
three days I will raise it up again. I
is the Spirit that quickeneth, the flesh
profiteth nothing ; the words that I have

spoken unto you are Spirit and are life."

Notwithstanding the declaration of Jesus, the Church that received his Truth has taken as its trust his literal flesh and blood, and the largest part of the Church claims by a perpetual miracle to constantly keep in stock a supply of the same. Jesus died to demonstrate that if we would take the Truth he taught and live the life he lived, we need not die. We call ourselves Christians, and yet so long as we are subject to sickness and death, we give the lie to our own profession. We have not yet learned the meaning of the words: " The kingdom of heaven is within." Our thoughts and hopes are still projected outwards. The Fire of Immortal Life was made manifest by a true prophet of God, but the Church that received it, like " She," was not in a fit state of mind for its perfect work. It gave outward form and power rather than inward truth and love.

When " She " first unveiled to Holly, she
seemed to say: " Behold me, lovely as no
woman was or is, undying and half divine ;
memory haunts me from age to age, and
passion leads me by the hand ; evil have I
done, and with sorrow have I made ac-
quaintance from age to age, and from age
to age evil I shall do, and sorrow shall I
know till my redemption comes."

Behold the Church, lovely as no other
power ever was or is. Egypt, Babylon,
Persia, Greece, Rome—none of the mighty
empires of the past are to be compared to
her. All that is best among all the living,
growing nations of the modern world is of
the Church : the finest buildings in all our
cities, the free gifts of loving hearts; her
spires the jewels in every landscape; her
charities smoothing the pillows of the sick,
comforting with hope the dying, caring for
widow and orphan. Her truth, though
clouded with error, giving wing to the

loftiest flights of genius, pathos to sublim-
est utterances of oratory, most entrancing
harmonies to music, and noblest themes to
art. And yet, passion has debased her
love. Cruel death in dungeon, at the
stake, in civil strife and awful carnage, are
the evils she has done. Watching through
the ages for the resurrection of her Lord—
his return in glory and triumph—in doubt
and denial—has been her sorrow.

As came the redemption of "She," even
so shall come that of the Church. How did
it come?—through Leo and Holly.

We are told that, outwardly, Holly was
as ugly as Leo was handsome. One was
called The Greek God, the other Charon, the
Boatman of The Styx. By the wild people
over whom "She" ruled one was called
Lion, and the other Baboon. Holly was the
guardian of Leo.

Who are these two? Let me tell you:
one is *Science;* the other *Intuition.*

A short time after Leo was born Holly received him in charge, also a mysterious casket, from the child's father. The father of Intuition is Conscience. Holly was the friend of Leo's father—so Science has been the friend of Conscience. In the knowledge of the past, obtained by loyalty to external intellect, Science had in its keeping (a long time before it knew the meaning of the possession) the few hints of Truth that will yet guide it, together with Intuition, to the redemption of the Church and of the world. Though Holly was outwardly ugly, yet he was at heart true and honest. So is Science in its proper sphere. It has tried through the theory of evolution to relate us to a monkey form, and would have succeeded but for Intuition, which has brought back to us the knowledge of our royal ancestry, our Divine parentage.

Our author says: " There appears to be nothing in the character of Leo Vincey which, in the opinion of most people, would have been likely to attract an intellect so powerful as that of ' She.' But the explanation of this is that 'She,' seeing further than we can see, perceived the germ and smouldering spark of greatness which lay hidden within her lover's soul, and well knew that under the influence of her gift of life, watered by her wisdom and shone upon with the sunshine of her presence, it would bloom like a flower and flash out like a star, filling the world with fragrance and light."

This is most prophetically true, and that flower is now at the bud. Some who can see with prophetic vision have, like the wise men of the East, already beheld that star.

When the mysterious box was opened, Holly cast discredit upon the whole thing; but Leo immediately resolved to go, and at any cost solve the mystery. In spite of every difficulty, of every doubt cast upon the probability of the truth of the strange

story by Holly, Leo never doubted it for a
moment. He knew it was true and always
expected to find the object of their search.
It was a strange inheritance : A fragment
of pottery, a weird story of a glorious and
royal ancestry, and one solitary jewel, bear-
ing the legend *The Royal Son of the Sun.*

Such is the mysterious inheritance of the
children of Intuition to-day. A fragment
of truth from out the past that carries
us back to Egypt—" Out of Egypt have I
called my son." A jewel bearing a device
whose full meaning we have not yet fath-
omed—" Now are we the children of **God**,
and it is not yet made manifest what we
shall be." To the righteous God is a sun—
to the wicked, a consuming fire. This is the
Fire of Life—the baptism of Love and Truth
—but before we bathe in it we must be sure
we are ready. A few to-day have laid these
things to heart, and have actually accepted
them. Faith is not yet dead on the earth.

Under the heroic constancy and devotion of Science to Truth, Intuition has grown from childhood to youth. He has been made acquainted with the splendor and marvellous possibilities of his inheritance. Together with Science, his faithful guardian, he has started on the eventful journey that is to clear up the mystery surrounding it. This is well. Intuition must not despise Science They must journey together. They have in the past been divorced. Leo's father—that is, Conscience—went on this same enterprise alone, and, as a consequence, returned defeated, and yet he went far enough, in what he saw and heard, to strengthen his faith. After this, he married a beautiful bride (Religious Enthusiasm), from which union, at the cost of his mother's life, Leo was born. Unable to endure the sight of the child, the father sought, through study, to gain the knowledge the absence of which rendered abortive his attempt to penetrate the mystery of his inheritance. But the hand of death was upon him, and, before dying, he made the arrangements that in-sured a partnership between his son Leo (Intuition) and his new friend Holly (Science). In the past there have been many failures through the lack of this union. How many, with some light of Intuition, have failed to read the full meaning of life through discarding Science. This was the weakness of the Church in the spiritual awakening at the birth of Methodism. When the enthusiasm and power of the Spirit was upon it Science was treated as an enemy instead of an ally. At the birth of Unitarianism Channing almost united the two, but leaned a little too much on Science, while his succeessors have leaned more and more until the majority of them prefer Science to faith. But for the enthusiasm and faith of Leo, Holly would have stayed in the comfortable cloisters of Cambridge. So

we find many hugging the delights of cult-
ure and the seclusion of the scholar's life,
instead of making the heroic attempt to re-
generate the Church and the world. Some
who have espoused this cause in the name
of Christian Science are also leaning more
upon Science than Intuition, preferring
Holly to Leo. All is Mind, they affirm,
and forget Love; and so, instead of union,
we find separation—instead of faith leading
onward to redemption, doubt is retarding
the great movement. As Emerson says:
" If in your metaphysics you have denied
personality to the Deity ; yet, when the de-
vout emotions of the soul come, yield to
them, heart and life, though they should
clothe God with shape and color, leave
your theory, as Joseph his coat in the hand
of the harlot, and flee."

Some, like Swedenborg, have gone half
way into the mysterious continent, but have
never penetrated to the centre. Had Leo

gone no further after he met Ustane he would have been the representative of many a true son of Intuition, like Swedenborg and Andrew Jackson Davis.

When the storm swept Leo from the boat it was Holly's strong hand that rescued him. Intuition needs Science and Science needs Intuition.

Holly and Leo were accompanied by a faithful servant, Job, who symbolizes practical every-day life. There is a strong temptation to start out on this search without such a companion. Many who have caught a glimpse of the glory of our spiritual inheritance have thrown prudence to the winds, and neglected every suggestion and service of common-sense and experience. These, like Job, keep us in sight of fear; still the time has not yet come when we can dispense with their useful service. We cannot yet make our bread as Jesus fed the multitude, pay our taxes by catching a fish with a piece of money in its mouth, nor walk on the water instead of employing a boat.

After Leo and Holly reached the Fire of Life Job died in the presence of the stupendous miracle. The time is coming when we shall be sufficiently spiritual to be master over all material conditions. Until it does come let us not delay the redemption of "She" by neglecting to be practical. Do not promise to restore an arm that has been cut off. You can safely say the time will soon be here when such things will be done, even as Jesus restored the ear cut off by Peter and raised the dead—"Be ye wise as serpents and harmless as doves."

Children of the Sun and of the Lion-heart, much depends on our prudence as well as our courage. We know that our Redeemer liveth. We know that the word of God is true and shall not return unto Him void. We know that we shall solve

at last the great Mystery of Life and con-
quer our last enemy—Death. We know
that the Truth shall make us free. But the
way that leadeth into life is straight and
narrow—yea, rough and difficult, as sym-
bolized in the experiences of Leo and Holly
on board the ship off the African coast,
surrounded with traitors, dashed by a sudden
storm into the howling waves of the sea,
saved by their own life-boat — but how
thrilling the danger : "Above the awful
shriekings of the hurricane came a duller,
deeper roar. Great heavens! It was the
voice of breakers! At that moment the
moon began to shine forth, out far across
the torn bosom of the ocean shot the
ragged arrows of her light, and there, half
a mile ahead of them, was a white line of
foam, then a little space of open-mouthed
blackness, and then another line of white.
It was the breakers, and their roar grew
clearer and yet more clear as they sped

down upon them like a swallow. There they were, boiling up in snowy spouts of spray, smiting and gnashing together like the gleaming teeth of hell."

All who reach the Fire of Life must get through these breakers. They are the cruel interpretations of orthodoxy, a barbarous ideal of God, a physical passion and blood atonement, a theory of miracles inconsistent with Science, a false and belittling conception of man, a phariseeism that says " I am holier than thou," a love that does not shine for sinner (so-called) as well as saint—but time would fail me to name them all. Their name is Legion. The whole country of "She" is infested with them.

What carried our brave adventurers through? Not the courage of Leo (Intuition). He was helpless in the bottom of the boat, just rescued from death by the iron grip of Holly (Science). What saved them? The practical service of Job and the experience of one of the crew of their ship, the only surviver. Whom does he represent? Scepticism—sheer Infidelity. Practical service and the absolute defiance and daring of the sceptic can alone carry us through those breakers, and yet many think that the infidel has no place in God's world.

Does not the sun shine and the rain fall for him also? When we recognize ourselves as God's children our love will include him. The Church will never be redeemed without him. He is helping us through those awful breakers—those gleaming teeth of hell. Let your love sustain him in his rough work. Be grateful for his splendid courage of denial and preference for no God to one with the instincts of a savage. He, poor brave fellow, has but a short time to live. When captured by the savages over whom "She" ruled, they attempted to hotpot him. The protection of "She" did not extend to him, for her message spoke only

of white men and he was black. While
trying to protect him from this awful fate
he was shot dead by Holly. So Science
will yet destroy, in seeking Truth, the very
life of Infidelity. It has almost done this
already. There are but few survivors of
his school of thought. Every one with
the slightest penetration sees that Science is
trembling on the verge of discoveries, in its
awful struggle with ignorance and super-
stition, that will utterly slay Infidelity and
Materialism.

After the breakers are past, our voyagers
meet with a pleasant experience. They
enter the mouth of a quiet river—" Only
heaving gently like some troubled woman's
breast, giving them leisure to reflect upon
all they had gone through and all they
had escaped. The moon went slowly
down in chastened loveliness. She de-
parted like some sweet bride into her
chamber, and long, veil-like shadows crept

up the sky through which the stars peeped shyly out. Soon, however, they too began to pale before a splendor in the east, and then the quivering footsteps of tne dawn came rushing across the new born blue and shook the planets from their places. Quieter and yet more quiet grew the sea, quiet as the soft mist that brooded on her bosom and covered up her troubling as the illusive wreaths of sleep brood upon a pain-racked mind, causing it to forget its sorrow. From the east to the west sped the angels of the dawn—from sea to sea—from mountain top to mountain top—scattering light with both their hands. On they sped out of the darkness, perfect, glorious, like spirits of the just breaking from the tomb—on over the quiet sea—over the low coastline and the swamps beyond and the mountains beyond them; over those who slept in peace and those who woke in sorrow; over the evil and the good; over the living and the dead; over the wide world and all that breathes or has breathed thereon. It was a wonderfully beautiful sight and yet sad, perhaps from the very excess of its beauty."

The arising sun, the setting sun, even so shall this rest and refreshing this bitter-sweet—this sad joy—be ours. Once pass the breakers of false belief, and peace that passeth understanding shall give you rest.

" As one whom his mother comforteth, so will I comfort you," is the promise.

You are about to land on the continent of " She " to penetrate to the mystery of truth. This country seems at first lighted by the moon only —the reflected rays from a sun of faith that has set. Even this goes down and the stars, the dim lights of other faiths, like Mohammedanism and Zoroastrianism, and Buddhism, fade away. Why? Because a new sun is rising. Already the *avant couriers*—the first rays of clearer

truth, are chasing away the night, and a long
bar of light flushes the east.

> "For, look, the morn, in russet mantle clad,
> Walks o'er the dew of yon high eastward hill."

Leo revives. Leo lives. Hope is new-
born—Intuition is saved. Once again the
soul speaks to man and proclaims its one-
ness with God. Emerson said:

> "If but one hero knew it,
> The world would blush in flame;
> The sage till he hit the secret
> Would hang his head in shame."

But at last a hero knows it. A sage has
hit the secret. The light is here and shame
no longer sits on the brow of highest truth.
Reader, do you not feel the breath of this
new morn? Awake—awake thou that sleep-
est. It is time to live and work. A long
journey—a great task—many dangers—and
a mighty rescue are before us.

Our travellers now penetrate the interior.
Their path is one of utmost danger and dis-

comfort. Think not, therefore, because a new life of ecstacy has thrilled you with burning enthusiasm that your work is done, your mission achieved. Ah, no—it has only just begun. How many have made this mistake, and so, when the night has come again, their courage failed them and they fell by the way. Press on, press on, ye children of rescue, "She" waits your coming. And you, O, brothers and sisters in the world of sense—lost in the night, living in tombs—wait, wait a little longer, for we are on the road and nothing shall stay us.

Our travellers' way lay along a river bordered with swamps, inhabited by wild beasts of prey. At day they are scorched by a burning sun; at night tortured with myriads of insects. Think you, my heroic comrades, we can escape the scorching fires of unfriendly criticism—the stinging tongues of slander—the attacks of the wild beasts of passion and sensuality? Like Leo, we are

ready and willing to die for Truth. We
have said we are dead to flesh and alive to
spirit. Can we yet say "It is finished?"
Take heed.—This is to him who think-
eth he standeth. Watch and pray, lest ye
enter into temptation. "Many are called
but few are chosen." Remember the in-
scription on the gates of Busyrane—" Be
bold ";and on the second gate—" Be bold,
be bold, and 'evermore be bold "; but on the
third gate—" Be not too bold." The no-
blest courage must be armored with discre-
tion.

Our travellers are now captured by the
savages over whom " She " rules. They
would have been slain but for the command
of " She," who has foreseen their coming
and charged Bellali, the Father of the Tribe,
to protect their lives.

Bellali represents the Priesthood. The
more ignorant and superstitious would, long
ago, have crushed out Science and Intui-

tion, but for the fact that many of the clergy have felt an impression that the Church had need of them.

Our travellers are now taken into one of the tombs, in which these people live. They would instantly have been hot-potted but for the command of " She," as thousands, with like courage and devotion to truth, have been. At last we may seek truth and not be physically tortured, though a good many think that this is only an experience that yet awaits us in another life.

While waiting to learn the further will of " She," Leo's brave and handsome form wins for him the love of the beautiful savage maiden Ustane, who, according to the custom of the country, selects him for her husband with a kiss. Ustane represents a movement closely allied to the Church, and yet strangely differing from it; I mean modern Spiritualism. At present Spiritualism and Intuition are closely allied. We

shall find that we are to be greatly in-
debted to this movement. Its character and
destiny are most accurately symbolized
by Ustane. Ustane was physically beauti-
ful, possessed great devotion to Leo, de-
fended his life at the risk of her own, gifted
with prophecy and yet not understanding
the meaning of her visions, sensible of the
brevity of her life in daring to love Leo and
yet defying death for love. When Leo
was neglected by "She," Ustane watched
faithfully by his side. When driven forth
by the command of *She who must be obeyed*,
she preferred to return and die in the sight
of her Leo, than to remain absent from his
side. At first Holly saves her life by re-
minding "She" that but for her devotion
Leo would have been slain ; but when Us-
tane disobeys and returns to contest the
place by Leo's side with "She," her fate is
sealed, and the mighty power of the silent
will of " She " strikes her dead at Leo's feet,

Even in this awful moment, when Leo, maddened with the desire for vengeance, rushes to take the life of Ustane's murderess, her mighty power hurls him back without effort, and in a few minutes he is at her feet, vowing eternal love, while " She " exclaims :

" I have waited and my reward is with me ; I have overcome Death and Death brought back to me him that was dead, therefore do I rejoice ; for fair is the future, green are the paths that we shall tread across the everlasting meadows. The hour is at hand. Night hath fled away into the valleys ; the dawn kisseth the mountain tops, soft shall we lie, my love, and easy shall we go. Crowned shall we be with the diadem of kings. Worshipping and wonder struck, all peoples of the world, blinded, shall fall before our beauty and our might. From time unto time shall our greatness thunder on, rolling like a chariot through

the dust of endless days, laughing shall we
speed in our victory and pomp, laughing
like the daylight as he leaps along the hills
—onward, still triumphant to a triumph
ever new; onward, in our power to a power
unattained ! Onward, never weary, clad
with splendor for a robe. Till accomplished
be our fate, and the night is rushing down."

All this is wonderful—marvellous—in
the aptness of its symbolism and prescience.
Before the Church thought of recognizing
Intuition, Spiritualism fell in love with its
beauty, only "She" put it to a phenomenal
instead of a spiritual use. This wild and
savage creature, lawless and unconventional,
free and bold in her love, has yet defended
with her life the right to a present inspira-
tion—thrusting her own body between In-
tuition and the threatening spears of dog-
matic ecclesiastical condemnation. For her
right to live, many of the representatives of
science have pleaded—not seeing that

either Spiritualism or the Church must
die, and that short and feeble must be the
struggle of the former for supremacy. Al-
ready Spiritualism feels in anticipation the
night rushing down on her, but she will re-
sist and defy the Church for a time. Then
Inspiration will forsake her. Already those
of her lovers in whom Inspiration has
ripened into Intuition are at the feet of
" She," going back into the ministry or
taking up with Theosophy, Rosicrucianism,
Hermetic Philosophy, or the new ministry
of Christian Science. We mourn the fate
of Ustane, and yet we see that only can she
ever truly live by dying. The rainbow of
hope encircles her dying moments as she
exclaims, " Ay, I die—I die and go into the
darkness, nor know I whither I go! But
this I know: There is a light shining in
my breast, and by that light, as by a lamp
I see the truth and the future. When first
I knew my Lord I knew also that death

would be the bridal gift he gave me—it
.rushed upon me of a sudden—but I turned
not back, being ready to pay the price; and
behold, death is here! And now—even as
I knew that—so do I, standing on the steps
of doom, know that thou shalt not reap the
profits of thy crime. Mine he is, and
though thy beauty shine like a sun among
the stars, mine shall he remain. For thee
—never here in this life shall he look thee
in the eyes and call thee spouse. Thou
too art doomed!"—Ustane saw no further;
because the power of "She" slew her.

As Leo was the reincarnation of Kalli-
krates so was Ustane the expression of
Amenartas. Before, Kallikrates lost his
life because he had set the love of his heart
on the dying instead of the undying—the
Psychic instead of the Spiritual. Now,
Ustane dies to save Leo because our love
must be entirely spiritual. Spiritualism
pleases but does not elevate. It is a garden

of rare and beautiful flowers, some of which are deadly poison, and yields no fruit unto Righteousness. Theosophy and other kindred movements are only the passing thrills of vengeance in Leo's breast. He longed to sweep " She " from the face of the earth. Already they are retiring before the mighty power of "She." But " She " also must lose her outward form, for that too is of the earth earthy, and though two thousand years it has defied the encroachments of time, it too is doomed. Before " She " knew that her love had returned—was actually in her abode—she was entirely taken up with Holly, though Leo was struggling in the very jaws of death. Even so is it with the Church. She gives hospitality to Science, shows him much courtesy, while Intuition is almost dying, left as he is solely to Spiritualism and practical Service, as Leo was left to Ustane and Job. Already the Church is trying to shape her Theology to the demands of Science. The doctrine of our Baboon origin is preached in many a pulpit and tolerated in many of her colleges. Science has for a little time appropriated the place of Intuition. Holly, in one of his interviews with " She," had on his hand the ring belonging to Leo containing the scarab on which was the motto, " The Royal Son of the Sun." In the delirium of fever Leo had dropped it and Holly picked it up and thoughtlessly put it on. Science has received such a warm welcome from " She " that he actually thinks he is born of the sun and will be her lover, knowing not that " She " cannot for a moment really entertain his love. But "She" is something of a coquette. So is the Church, and hence she feigns love to Science, knowing in her heart of hearts she yet waits her true lord. As " She " catches sight of the scarab a new emotion shoots through all her being. " Man," she half-whispered, half-hissed, throwing back her head like a snake about to strike,—" Man, where didst thou get that scarab on thy hand! Speak, or by the spirit of life, I will blast thee where thou standest." Poor Holly was so frightened that he fell on the ground before her—babbling out that he picked it up—forgetting in his terror that it belonged to Leo. So, let the Church get the first sign from her risen Lord, and through all her form will course a stream of life and power before which Science will be dumb with amazement. And yet, think how near we are to this day when her Lord *is* here—only " She " does not know it. The Christ (Truth) is born again. The Soul has spoken. The sick are healed. The blind receive their sight. Devils are cast out. Soon the dead will be raised. The age of miracles is again at the very doors of the Church. Beautiful, God-like Intuition has been smitten by her own ignorant subjects, and poisoned with the malaria arising from the swamps of their hypocrisy and superstition, and all this time "She" is coquetting with Science. The lion-hearted, who have dared all for Truth,—even to accepting the love of Ustane—are almost perishing from neglect. Oh! Church, worship no longer at the tomb of a dead Lord when a living one needs your help! Stop exhibiting your corpses, and recounting the strange marvels of the dead past to the scrutiny of Science.

At last, pity takes "She" to the bedside of poor Leo and she beholds her love in the very throes of death. For a little time it is uncertain whether the remedy she administers is not too late. During that awful moment of suspense she suffers indescribable agony. At last the scale turns in favor of life. For two thousand years had "She" lived without companionship, without comfort, without death, led on down her dreary road by the marsh lights of hope

which, though they flickered here and there,
and now glowed strong and now were not,
yet the spirit of prophecy assured her that
her deliverer would come.

" Then, think of it," "She" says, "Oh
Holly — for never shalt thou hear such
another tale or see such another scene—
nay, not even if I give thee ten thousand
years of life, and thou shalt have it in pay-
ment if thou wilt. Think, at last my de-
liver came—he for whom I had watched and
waited through the generations—at the ap-
pointed time he came to seek me as I knew
that he must come, for my wisdom could
not err, though I knew not when or how—
yet see how ignorant I was! See how small
my knowledge and faint my strength! For
hours he lay sick unto death and I felt it
not—I who had waited for him two thousand
years—I knew it not."

Even so is it with the Church to-day. In
spite of her wondrous antiquity, so rich and

yet so poor, so wise and yet so ignorant, so mighty and yet so weak, her Deliverer is here. He for whose return she has watched for two thousand years—renewing again and again the flickering light of Hope—and lo, now Knowledge is born and she is ignorant. Now Love is here to take her as his Bride and she still hates. Courage is here and she still fears. Faith is here and she still doubts. The grave has given up its dead and she still sits weeping therein.

Who can describe the joy of " She " when Leo was fully recovered? It was indeed her redemption. Nothing can rescue the Church from its night of weary watching but the light of Intuition companioned by Spiritualized Science.

When Leo gave to " She " love for love and grace for grace, she exclaimed: " I swear, even in this first most holy hour of completed womanhood, that I will abandon evil and cherish good. I swear that I will

be ever guided by thy voice in the straight-
est path of duty. I swear that I will eschew
Ambition and through all my length of
endless days set Wisdom over me as a
guiding star to lead me unto Truth and a
knowledge of the Right. I swear also that
I will honor and will cherish thee, Kalli-
krates, who hast been swept by the wave of
time back into my arms. Ay, till the very
end, come it soon or late, I swear—nay, I
will swear no more, for what are words?
Yet shalt thou learn that Ayesha hath no
false tongue."

In this sublime spirit—in this complete
consecration, sacrifice and service, thrilling
with the baptism of this all radiant and per-
fect love, "She" enters the bath of fire, and
lo, instead of preserving, it destroys. But
Holly and Leo live. They imbibe enough
of the fire to experience its exhilarating
potency. "She" is enshrined in the heart
of Leo, and also of Holly, though the mantle

of " She " falls through the gloom of the
night upon Leo.

No words are yet born that can fully de-
scribe the meaning of all this. The bath
of fire is the cleansing power of Spirit—
the recognition that we are not flesh and
blood but spirit, is to bathe therein. The
death of " She " and the salvation of Leo
means that living Intuition—the open vision
of Truth with the last veil torn away—is to
take the place of the dead dogmas—the
corpses of the past—with which the Church,
like " She " has so long illumined the night
of her darkness. The outward form of
" She " perished, but her spirit was new
born—for the letter killeth but the Spirit
giveth life.

As Leo and Holly both live, so shall
Science and Intuition work together as one.
Religion is to become scientific and Science
religious. The Church shall be redeemed.
The Church shall serve the Truth with all

her wealth and power. The old forms shrivel up in the cleansing fires of Truth and Love—but new and more beautiful ones will soon be born. It is faith makes us (as Emerson says)—not we it. It is the soul saves us—not we the soul. We have but to love and serve—to conquer fear—to go forth like Holly and Leo to solve our mystery and find our inheritance, and lo, whatever our dangers, we shall be delivered from them all. "He shall give His angels charge concerning thee." "Fear not little flock, for it is your Father's good pleasure to give you the kingdom." "Knock and it shall be opened—seek and ye shall find."

So went I forth and found. Smitten by the storm of doubt I sank into the black depths of infidelity. I was saved as by a miracle—the strong hand of science and the courage and daring that preferred no God to a lie, and the unselfishness of helpfulness to my great Human Brotherhood rather than believe that one could be lost. I saw the bright streamers of a new day chase away the shadows of the night, and the calm of toleration stilling the troubled waters of dogmatic fury. Though the arrows of slander robbed me of rest, the wild beasts of passion raved, and the scorching sun of criticism fevered my blood, yet I drew nearer, day by day to my beloved. In hours of danger " She" herself sent me succor. I was rescued from the fires of cruelty by the love of one I met by the way. Sweet were the dreams and joyous the hours she gave me. I forgot danger in the love of Ustane. Her devotion plucked me from the yawning gulf of death. It shielded me from the sharp spear of savage bigotry. But in the struggle for life before this deliverance I had received many a wound, and with the loss of blood I was faint. The malaria rising from the swamps of hypocrisy through which I passed made the blood boil in my veins and frenzied my brain with delirium. I lay in the very house of my beloved, struggling with death, neglected and forgotten. "She" at last saw me, and lo, I was the one she had waited for through the ages. How strong her hand to the rescue. How mighty her joy. How swift the action of her restorative. At first she seemed to me only as a ghost of the past. I turned to my Ustane, and " She" struck her a corpse at my feet. I raised my hand to be avenged and behold ! the might of her silent thought unnerved me. In the very presence of death, she unveiled her beauty, and I fell at her feet and knew that I had found my Queen, and my Beloved. The dead image of me, worshipped so long, was consumed. I drew from the face of Truth the last thin veil, and lo, she was mine. But the fire of this great love consumed her form, and, for a little while, she lived only in Heaven and the shrine of my heart. But

I know she will come back to me, more glorious than before. The light of prophecy illumines the future. No more will " She," dwell in tombs. No more will " She," worship the dead. No more will "She," mingle curses with her blessings, nor evil with her good. The tree of knowledge, of good and evil is cut down and the tree of life that *all is good* planted in its place.

Wherever man lives and toils, thinks and loves there dwells " She." From her Palace Beautiful lead all the highways of service. Beneath her smile hate flees from the world. War is a lost art. Poverty is unknown. The wild beasts have become gentle as lambs. The swamps are changed into smiling valleys. The mountains have bowed their heads and come down, while from foot to summit rise the terraces of fruitfulness. The elements are at peace. Spring and Summer are over all the earth ; Sickness has given all her place to Health ; Insanity to

Sanity ; Death to Life, for behold, when my Beloved returns in her beauty and strength, there is to be a new heaven and a new earth, and all things are to be made new.

EPILOGUE.

THE production of the foregoing inter-
pretation of "She," is something of a psy-
chological enigma to the writer. This re-
markable book was first read to while away
the hours on a long ocean voyage. Apart
and distinct from other books read for the
same purpose it seemed at one with the
music and mystery of the ocean, and to call
forth thoughts akin to those the everlasting
stars whisper to us when we invoke their
confidence.

To tell the truth I fell in love with "She,"
I dreamed of her by night and thought of
her by day. I felt as we have sometimes
felt when we suddenly meet a stranger,
whom, in an instant, we feel we have

always known, and go searching through the
corridors of the mind trying to remember
where and how we had met before.

I had always known " She," Where?
When ? How ? Did "She " really live,
and was I " Leo?"

I was quite sure that all this had a spiritual
meaning. In moments of inspiration I
caught glimpses of the truth and resolved to
unravel the mystery. The time, however,
was not yet ripe. I had already passed
through many of the experiences portrayed
in this interpretation, still I was no more
prepared to solve the mystery then than
Leo and Holly would have been, had they
gone no farther than the first cave—in
which Leo won the love of Ustane. I, also,
had my Ustane. " She " showed me things
of rarest beauty and I seemed to be in a
land of enchantment. All sense was more
highly gratified than in the world from
which I came. I saw with other eyes, heard

with other ears, was fed from an invisible source, enjoyed exquisite odors sweeter than any perfume of earth, and felt the touch and thrilling presence of unseen forms. In the language of Browning's " Paracelsus," I might say:

If some mortal born too soon
Were laid away in some great trance,
The ages coming and going all the while till dawned
His true time's advent and could then record
The words they spoke—who kept watch by his bed
Then I might tell more of the breath so light
Upon my eyelids, and the fingers warm
Among my hair.

Ah, the first joy of it! To feel that death has not robbed you of your beloved; to know that life is Lord of death! You tread upon enchanted ground. You sink into dreams of bliss on beds of flowers, and wake with a kiss upon your lips from an angel presence. You rise to pursue it that you may catch and hold it, and like a will-o'-the-wisp it eludes your grasp, until, blinded and bewildered, you fall into a morass, or find yourself plunged into some deadly spiritual conflict, faintly portrayed in the terrible struggle for existence which Holly and Leo underwent in this stage of their journey. The world of Psychic phenomena is indeed an enchanted realm, but woe to him who mistakes it for Paradise. Rest there, but sleep not. Refresh yourself, and in that strength, seek the true spiritual realm of which it is only a fair promise and prophecy.

Some of my readers will doubtless be inclined at first to rebel at the place assigned to Spiritualism in this wonderful allegory. But, oh, my brothers and sisters, you who have with me basked in the light of this fairy world and groped amid its shadows, the very profundity of your disappointment is the divine love and truth calling you to seek the true spiritual realm in which there is no night; for

" Night's candles are burnt out, and jocund day,
Stands tip-toe on the misty mountain tops."

How bewildering, how perplexing, the
frauds and cheats; how contradictory the
most inspired utterances of most gifted
mediumistic inspiration; how vague, how
wordy, often insipid and void of all conti-
nuity. · · Is this the world's full-orbed
hope? No—No. It is but some meteor
that the true sun exhales to be to our night
a torchbearer until the morning of a perfect
day dawns clear and bright. Tis time.

New hopes should animate the world, new light
Should dawn from new revealings to a race
Weighed down so long, forgotten so long ; so shall
The heaven reserved for us at last receive
Creatures whom no unwonted splendors blind,
But ardent to confront the unclouded blaze
Whose beams not seldom blessed their pilgrimage.
Not seldom glorified their life below.

To kindle in other minds this hope—to
point the way to the true fire of life is the
one wish of the writer. The way is straight

and narrow—full of difficulty, and yet if we are but brave of heart conquering fear, victory is sure. Who would not dare all for such a prize? Remember "faint heart never won fair lady." It was only *after* I had found my beloved that I knew the meaning of " She."

While yet the riddle was unsolved, I met one who had found the solution in his own life, and, strange to say, also attempted an interpretation of "She," finding the correspondence between her and the church. This he afterwards published in one of the New York magazines. It is quite distinct, with a value unique and instructive, but separate from the following, save in the one parallelism between " She "and the church.

I find it impossible to say whether or not I am indebted to that writer for this suggestion, as at the time, I knew not how to use it. In another way he gave me the key that opened the one closed chamber in my heart which was shutting out the perfect light of truth—by bringing me a message from the one who gave me the clue that unravels all mystery. The joy of this discovery is not to be told in words. The external mind that sticks to facts and the common place is pushed aside and made to act simply as amanuensis to the soul. That which I have told and would yet reveal can only be hinted at, sketched in rudest outline in symbol allegory as it rushes forth in rejoicing song and symbol.

Faith is almost dead in the world and hope's pinions droop; yet the night fleeth and the morning cometh. Soon we can sing :

> " The year's at the spring,
>   And day's at the morn,
>   Morning's at seven,
>   The hill sides dew-pearled,
>   The lark's on the wing,
>   The snail's on the thorn,
>   God's in his heaven—
>   All's right with the world."

Through sunshine and shadow, calm and storm, the great globe with its living freight rushes onward to perfection. Through all my long and eager search for truth and right, I was mounting higher, though as I climbed round and round the Mount of Endeavor I was sometimes in the shadow and at others in the shine. Looking back one day over this circuitous route I blushed with shame at the thought of recommending to others this long and weary way. A great conviction swept over me that I had not yet solved the full mystery of my inheritance as " The Royal Son of the Sun." As I felt more keenly the pain and misery, the unrest and war of the world, realizing that " I *was* my brother's keeper," that never could I enter into final and complete rest without finding deliverance for all, my every thought and breath became a prayer for light on this problem. In response the

Soul sent me the one to whom I have referred and who said:

" You have but one thing more to do to find the deliverance you desire—you are standing at the very threshold of the temple Truth. Only one veil hangs between you and your everlasting bride and the sanctuary in which there is rest for all, and that veil none but your own hand can remove, nor rend in twain."

" What is that?" I cried.

" The flesh," she replied.

" I have long denied the flesh," I answered, " and acknowledge it only as the servant of the soul." " I know," she answered, " but the flesh profiteth *nothing*—you are depending on many external methods both in the physical and psychic realm instead of on Spirit alone. Both are idolatry."

As the word of truth lighted up my life, I discovered what great possessions I had here, and so for a time was very sorrowful.

After a severe struggle I cried with every fibre of my being : " let me have the truth though I die ! I know that I am immortal and can live and work in other spheres." The veil parted, and I stood once more face to face with Jesus of Nazareth, and found myself in a Christian temple. For a moment, in my bewilderment, I thought of flight Intellectual pride said, " What ! you who have outgrown Christianity into all religions to become again a Christian ! " As this thought flashed upon me the features of Jesus were suddenly changed into those of Buddha and he replied, " I also have many forms. There is but one way—I am the way, the truth and the life. As Buddha, I taught the salvation that comes of denial of sense ; as the Christ, the saving power of faith or affirmation of Spirit." Then I was left alone in the temple, and through all my consciousness streamed the cleansing fires of infinite Truth and Love. I found myself

saying, " It is finished. I am dead to the
physical self. The flesh profiteth nothing
—Spirit is all. I have been crucified, dead,
and buried, and still I live ; I also am 'the
way, the truth, and the life.' The same
mind that was in the Buddha and in the
Christ is also in me."

Each man his prison makes. We forge
our own chains. All that men and women
suffer is of their own making. The same
power that makes can unmake. There is
deliverance for all. The truth shall make
us free. The kingdom of heaven is within
—it comes not by observation. This is the
temple that is built silently, without sound.
This is the lost word—the creative power of
thought—which the Masonic and other
secret societies have lost and are trying to
find amid the rubbish of external symbols.
This is the elixir of life—the cup of the
Sangraal.

Vision followed vision. I was translated

to a vast system of subterranean dungeons. In my hand was a key that unlocked them all—the denial of flesh and the affirmation of Spirit. I was lost in the old labyrinths of the Egyptians. This truth fell like a golden thread from the heavens, held by the hand of the Christ, following which I escaped from all its bewildering mazes. I was dying of thirst. In my hands was placed the cup, drinking of which I knew I could never thirst again. I was in the bowers of Paradise, and lo, one more beautiful than "She" —the hope of all my hopes, the dream of all my dreams—stood by my side and then was not—only I felt her beauty and life absorbed into mine, as two drops of dew meet and mingle into one. I stood in the heart of a burning sun of Truth, and lo, *I knew the meaning of "She."* Like Holly and Leo I became sensible of a wild and splendid exhilaration, of a glorious sense of such a fierce intensity of Life that the most buoy-

ant moments of past strength seemed tame
and feeble in comparison. I laughed aloud
one minute and the next wept for joy. In
this lightness of heart and intoxication of
brain I felt as though all the varied genius
of which the human intellect is capable had
descended upon me. I could have spoken
blank verse of Shakespearian beauty; all
sorts of great ideas flashed through my
mind; it was as though the bonds of my
flesh had been loosened and left the spirit
free to soar to the empyrean of its native
power. The sensations that poured in
upon me are indescribable. I seemed to
live more keenly, to reach to a higher joy,
and sip the goblet of a subtler thought than
ever it had been my lot to do before. I was
another and most glorified self, and all the
avenues of the Possible were for a space
laid open to the footsteps of the Real.

The very day after this experience I went

by a seeming accident to the theatre and the play was " She."

Intellect cried out with *Horatio:*

> "O' day and night, but this is wondrous
>   strange"—

while the soul replied with *Hamlet:*

> "And therefore as a stranger give it welcome.
> There are more things in heaven and earth, Ho-
>   ratio,
> Than are dreamt of in your philosophy."

A strange thrill of some mysterious re-lationship to " She " took possession of my thoughts until it took form in a desire to-interpret its meaning. Resolving to make the attempt, I reasoned out what seemed to me a plausible solution, and one night sat down to write. The moment I did so I had the same intensity of feeling, and all that I had outlined in my mind was swept away like driftwood before a flood—all took dif-ferent and unexpected shape, and before I

arose, or felt the slightest sense of fatigue,
I had written the full interpretation.

If I am indebted at all to Dr. S—— it
came forth from the unconscious and im-
personal side of me that knows neither mine
nor thine, and I readily, in that oneness,
share with him whatever of merit or good or
service there is in these pages. That they
may help to redeem "She," the Church, and
through the Church the world, is my most
earnest prayer.

When is that Redemption to come?
"She" herself tells, when she says: "Ah,
if man would but see that hope is from with-
in and not from without."

Even so does every pulpit proclaim that
"The kingdom is within," and yet the vast
majority look for it from without.

But a few have unveiled Truth. Leo has
survived his task. Love and Truth have
met. The bridal day has come. The joy

that will thrill through the world to-morrow will be felt but never told.

In concluding my task I can only say that I have done what I could to be true to *Truth.* But all language is too poor in which to pay its wealth. All external things are but hints, types, shadows of the glory thereof. Truth says to each : I love them that love me ; and those that seek me diligently shall find me. Behold, I stand at the door, and knock : if any man hear my voice and open the door, I will come in to him, and will sup with him, and he with me. He that overcometh I will give to him to sit down with me in my throne, as I also overcame and sat down with my Father in his throne. He that hath an ear, let him hear what the Spirit saith to the churches.

LEO MICHAEL.

APPENDIX.

BELIEVING—yea, knowing—that all that is true and permanent is supernatural—that is, above what in our blindness we have called Nature—I am quite content to expose myself to the charge of superstition by relating what follows :

After completing the last page of the foregoing and sending it to the printer, I sat musing at my study table, when a strong impression came over me to open "The Perfect Way," lying with several other books before me. Yielding to this impulse, and opening it at random, I found I had turned to page 174, and the following passage riveted my attention. I find therein such a wonderful coincidence and confirmation of some of the thoughts unfolded in the " Interpretation of ' She,' " that I am impelled to quote it here for the benefit of the reader :

" That the time of the rising of the Celestial Virgin and of the rehabilitation of truth by the Woman-Messias of the Interpretation is near at hand, they who watch the " times," and the " heavens," may know by more than one token. To name but one: the sign Leo, which upon the Celestial Chart precedes the Ascension of the Woman, going before her as her herald, is the sign of the present Head of the Catholic Church. When assuming that title, he declared his office to be that of the " Lion of the Tribe of Judah," the domicile of the sun, the tribe appointed to produce the Christ. To the ascension of this constellation, preparing, as it were, the way of the Divine Virgin, the prophecy of Israel in Genesis refers:

Judah is a strong lion ; my Son, thou art gone up. The sceptre shall not be taken away from Judah till the coming of the messenger—or Shiloh —the expectation of the nations.

"And not only does the chief Bishop of the Church bear this significant name of the "Lion," but he is also the thirteenth of that name, and thirteen is the number of the Woman and of the lunar cycle, the number of Isis and of the Microcosm. It is the number which indicates the fulness of things and the consummation of the "Divine Marriage"—the At-one-ment of Man and God.

"Moreover, the arms of Leo XIII. represent a tree on a mount, between two triune lilies, and in the dexter chief point a blazing star, with the motto "*Lumen in Cœlo.*" What is this tree but the tree of Life; these lilies but the Lilies of the new Annunciation,—of the *Ave* which is to reverse the curse of *Eva?* What star is this, if not the star of the second Advent! History repeats itself only because all history is already written in heaven."

It is not to be supposed from the above that the Pope Leo is to be the redeemer of

" She.". The letter killeth but the Spirit giveth life. He, however, is a sign that the new heaven and new earth in which all things are to be made new is near at hand. '

The deeper meaning of " She," and Leo —the Divine Marriage—the fruit of the tree of life that shall heal the world's sickness—the second coming of Christ to the world—through a life of virgin purity whose symbol is the lily—and whose star is now leading the only true wisdom on the earth —will follow this Intrepretation when the time is ripe.

Written in truth and love for all my Brothers and Sisters lost in the night and crying for the light.

CATALOGUE

OF

Lovell's Household Library.

NUMERICAL LIST OF
Lovell's Household Library.

This admirable series of Popular Books is printed on heavier and larger paper than other cheap series, and is substantially bound in a handsome lithographed (blue and gold) cover.

The following are the earlier issues. The best works of new fiction will be added as rapidly as they appear.

FOR

MOTHERS AND DAUGHTERS

A BOOK FOR ALL WOMEN

AND A COMPLETE

GUIDE FOR THE HOUSEHOLD

BY

MRS. E. G. COOK, M.D.

ILLUSTRATED WITH NUMEROUS PLATES, EXPLANATORY OF THE TEXT

One volume, 12mo, cloth, gilt, price, $1.50.

FOR SALE BY

FRANK F. LOVELL & CO.,

142 & 144 Worth Street, New York.

JUST PUBLISHED.

A DICTIONARY

OF THE

ENGLISH LANGUAGE

Pronouncing, Etymological and Explanatory,

EMBRACING

Scientific and other terms, numerous familiar terms, and a copious selection of Old English words

BY

THE REV. JAMES STORMONTH,

AUTHOR OF

"ETYMOLOGICAL AND PRONOUNCING DICTIONARY OF THE ENGLISH LANGUAGE FOR SCHOOLS AND COLLEGES," ETC.

THE PRONUNCIATION CAREFULLY REVISED

BY

The Rev. P. H. PHELP, M.A., Cantab.

One Vol., 12mo, cloth, gilt, $1.75.

NEW YORK:

FRANK F. LOVELL & CO.,

142 & 144 Worth Street.

BY

M. GODIN,

FOUNDER OF THE FAMILISTÈRE AT GUISE; PROMINENT LEADER OF
INDUSTERIES IN FRANCE AND IN BELGIUM; MEMBER OF THE
NATIONAL ASSEMBLY.

Translated from the French

BY

MARIE HOWLAND,

1 vol., cloth, 12mo, illustrated, $1.50.

THE CONDITION

OF THE

WORKING CLASS IN ENGLAND

IN 1884.

With Appendix written 1886, and Preface 1887,

BY

FREDERICK ENGELS.

TRANSLATED BY

FLORENCE KELLEY WISCHNEWETZKY.

1 vol., 12mo, cloth, $1.25.

FRANK F. LOVELL & CO., 142 and 144 Worth St., New York.

BY MRS. HUMPHRY WARD.

ROBERT ELSMERE,

BY

MRS. HUMPHRY WARD,

Author of "Miss Bretherton," "Milly and Olly."

1 Vol., 12mo, Lovell's Library, No. 1188, 50 cents.

"A remarkable book. It is many years since a work of fiction has appeared which reflects with anything like the power and art of 'Robert Elsmere' the leading issues and characteristics of the time, especially in the higher planes of thought. . . . She has done what was lawful and wholly within the scope of her art, and she has done it with an ability, a versatility, a suppleness and vigor combined which entitle her book to be considered a work of true genius."—*New York Tribune.*

"One of the most remarkable novels ever written. . . Readers of great novels may promise themselves a very exceptional treat."—*Boston Beacon.*

"Comparable in sheer intellectual power to the best works of George Eliot. . . . Unquestionably one of the most notable works of fiction that has been produced for years."—*Scotsman.*

"We anticipate for 'Robert Elsmere' even a warmer reception here than it has had in England, for it is a great novel. It will attract the lovers of the best literature, because of its extreme literary power and charm, and it will gain the absorbed attention of all men and women."—*Literary World.*

"This is in many ways a remarkable novel, which has taken its place as undoubtedly the novel not of the year, but of the decade. Nothing, indeed, approaching it has appeared in its particular department since the last work of George Eliot."—*Churchman.*

"As an expression of the intellectual life of to-day, especially of that side of it which touches on science in its bearings on theology, it is a remarkable book . . . this artistic reticence is one of the qualities which make 'Robert Elsmere' one of the strongest works of fiction that have appeared in England since George Eliot."—*Critic.*

"In every respect the noblest and most notable novel that has been written in the English language since the publication of 'Daniel Deronda.'"—*Philadelphia Press.*

JOHN W. LOVELL COMPANY, NEW YORK.

THE
INTERNATIONAL MAGAZINE
OF
CHRISTIAN SCIENCE

Will be published the first of each month.

The intentions and objects of its publishers are:

FIRST — To teach the power of Mind.

To teach that true Religion and Science are identical.

To teach that true Religion and Health are synonymous.

To prove that Science understood will comfort and satisfy the people, bringing to them all the desires of their hearts.

SECOND. — To impress on the minds and hearts of the people the mighty truths of Christian Science, and the immediate importance of disseminating those truths and applying them in the minutest details of every-day life.

THIRD. — To have a strictly Christian Science Magazine which shall not overlook or cast aside people who are struggling into mental methods, even though they have not yet reached their highest possibilities.

FOURTH. — To present a complete review of the current news concerning the progress of Christian Science.

Purely Christian Science articles by leading scientists are promised from time to time. Foremost among these we name Mrs. Emma Hopkins, who will contribute Bible Lessons, answer questions, and give practical hints to students.

Correspondence by leading friends of the cause in all parts of the world.

MARY H. PLUNKETT, EDITOR.

TERMS:
In the United States and Canada.

One year, in advance,	$2.00
Single copy,	20

Miscellaneous Advertisements solicited; but none inconsistent with the basis and aims of Christian Science will be admitted under any circumstances or at any price.

All money orders, checks, etc., should be made payable to the order of the UNITY PUBLISHING COMPANY. Postage stamps, in payment for subscription or advertising, not acceptable.

Address all communications to

UNITY PUBLISHING COMPANY, 13 West 42d St., New York.

www.ingramcontent.com/pod-product-compliance
Lightning Source LLC
Chambersburg PA
CBHW020326090426
42735CB00009B/1423

* 9 7 8 3 3 3 7 0 1 9 8 5 3 *